LET YOUR VOICE BE HEARD

A Guide to Getting the Benefits You Earned and Deserve

by

Tammy James

Let Your VOICE Be Heard, A Guide to Getting the Benefits You Earned and Deserve, is a quick help guide that will help you to better understand and navigate the Veterans Benefits Administration (VBA) system. The Veterans Benefits Administration (VBA) is not the easiest to navigate. Many veterans are entitled to certain benefits, but never receive what they deserve. Every veteran is different. Every veteran has different medical conditions that may affect them differently. What applies to one person, even in the same war-time era or location may not apply to the next. In this book I will help you to navigate the VBA system and get the benefits you earned and deserve.

Required Documents Every Veteran Should Have

Every veteran should maintain a copy of his or her DD Form 214, which is the separation paperwork issued by each branch of the service. Depending on when you served, or if you served in the Guard or Reserves, you may have a similar form which has a different form name. Whichever form you have, keep a copy of it in a safe place, as it is the key to unlocking your benefits!

Copyright © [2019] by Tammy James

All rights reserved. No part of this book may be reproduced, scanned,

or distributed in any printed or electronic form without permission.

Printed in the United States of America

Written by Tammy James

Self- Published by Tammy James and Tacerra Fitchett

Photo Credit Sabrina Newby

(One Veteran Helping Another)

Table of Contents

Chapter 1 How can I be granted a service connection disability?

Chapter 2 What is a Fully Developed Claim and How to file?

Chapter 3 What is Special Monthly Compensation, and Do I qualify?

Chapter 4 What is a Clear and Unmistakable Error (CUE)?

Chapter 5 What is Dependency and Indemnity Compensation (DIC)?

Chapter 6 What is an appeal, and how long is the process?"

Chapter 7 What is Individual Unemployability?

Chapter 8 How do I file for Military Sexual Assault with little to no proof?

Chapter 9 How do I get my DD – 214?

Chapter 1 "How can I be granted a service connection disability?"

You can be granted a service connection disability for a direct service connection. For direct service connection you must have an illness or injury must have happened in military service. The illness must be documented in Service Medical Records (SMR's), and the illness or injury must be current. The Department of Veterans Affairs (DVA), will only compensate for injuries that are chronic and current. For example, a service member had an accident in service which resulted in a knee injury. It has caused ongoing pain and requires frequent visits to the pain clinic for treatment after getting out of the military. That injury is considered service - connected. If the illness or injury is fixed or cured at any point, even after you have been service connected, a reduction or total severance for that disability is possible as that condition is no longer chronic. Secondary conditions can only be established after a primary condition has been connected in order to receive compensation. VA is authorized to compensate eligible individuals only for "service connected" conditions. A service-connected condition is a condition caused by, aggravated by, or the result of, an event during military service or a condition considered service-connected by law (such as Section 1151 claims). As such, "service connection" is a critical concept in VA benefits law. The determination of service connection can be difficult and frustrating for the veteran.

Establishing service connection generally requires:

1. Medical evidence of a current disability or condition;

2. Evidence of an in-service occurrence or aggravation of a disease or injury; and

3. Medical evidence of either a nexus between the claimed in-service disease or injury and the current disease or injury.

As a practical matter, establishing the existence of a current medical condition or disability is usually straightforward because the condition is often the motivation for filing a claim. A past condition that has been corrected or resolved does not provide a basis for service connection.

Next, the condition must have occurred in or resulted from the veteran's military service. In most cases, the evidence of the event (wounded by enemy action, training injury) can be found in service records, service medical records, or unit records. Under certain circumstances, a claimant may establish an in-service event by other evidence, such as "buddy statements" or testimony by other service members witnessing the event or private medical records. Whatever the case, VA will also review service medical records to determine if the claimed condition existed when the veteran entered service. If a condition is determined to be "pre-existing" and not aggravated in service, the claim will be denied.

There are also certain "presumptions" regarding specific conditions and in-service events (Atomic Test Participation, Agent Orange, or Gulf War exposure) that may apply. A presumption is when the law assumes an event occurs except when there is evidence that the event did not happen. So, for veterans who were exposed to radiation during atomic bomb tests, that radiation is assumed to cause certain diseases? If the veteran now suffers from one of those diseases, he or she does not have to prove the radiation caused the disease: VA must accept that disease as service-connected.

Finally, VA must find a "nexus" (a "connection") between the current condition and the in-service disease, injury, or event. In practice, most service-connection issues boil down to whether a claimant can establish a nexus. For many medical conditions, such as cancer, it is extremely difficult to connect the current disease to specific events, even when occurrence of the event is not disputed. In such cases, it is especially important for the claimant to obtain strong medical evidence supporting nexus. This is not easy. Providing adequate nexus evidence becomes even more difficult as the time between service and the claim grows.

Although a condition must result from actions "in the line of duty," service-connected conditions are not limited to "battlefield" wounds or similar injuries. The "in the line of duty" requirement has been broadly interpreted to mean almost anything that occurs during service, including such things as car accidents, sports injuries, and illnesses unrelated to specific military activity. The condition generally need only have occurred or begun during service, including authorized leave periods.

Secondary Service Connection

"Secondary" service connection is awarded when a disability "is proximately due to or the result of a service-connected disease or injury." Proximate cause is defined as that which, in a natural and continuous sequence, unbroken by any efficient intervening cause, produces injury, and without which the result would not have occurred.

Example: you can file for primary and secondary conditions at the same time, but if the primary condition is denied, then the secondary will more than likely be denied as well. For example, a gulf war veteran is currently connected for three injuries. He would like to get service connected for Sleep disturbance. He did not receive a sleep study while in service and was previously denied through direct service connection. Although he cannot get a direct service connection for Sleep disturbance, he decides to get it linked to a condition he is already connected for as a secondary condition. A secondary condition must be a result (or aggravation) of a primary condition. Aggravation of a preservice disability is when the veteran is presumed in sound condition when examined, accepted, and enrolled for service, except as to defects, infirmities, or disorders noted at the time of the examination. You can sometimes receive compensation benefits for a pre-existing condition if you had the medical condition before you served in the military and your condition worsened during your military service. If this applies, you can be eligible for service - connected disability compensation based on "aggravation of a preservice disability." Don't panic if the initial service connection attempt is denied because it existed at the time of your entry into military service. The claim will have to be properly developed in such a way as to prove aggravation. As an example, a veteran starts a claim for bi - lateral pes planus (or flat feet). He was seen for flat feet multiple times throughout military service and now must wear inserts to alleviate pain due to his collapsed arches. His asymptomatic bi - lateral pes planus was annotated on his entrance exam. His claim is denied, "due to the natural progression of the condition" says the VA. You will typically see this reasoning when there is nothing in the claim specifying at which point the injury / illness worsened. Proving aggravation can be tricky, but it is possible. Presumptive Conditions are on the VA's list of conditions that are presumed to be related to service. Veterans do not have to prove that their current medical condition is related to their military service; the law presumes it. A presumptive condition can transmute through wartime or peacetime OR stateside or overseas. If the claim is received by VA after one year of release from active duty, the effective date is the date of receipt of the claim or when the date entitlement arose, whichever is later. Service Connection due to Injury Caused by treatment in the VA Health Care System is less common. If a veteran is injured because of VA hospitalization, treatment, rehab or therapy, the injury is automatically treated as service - connected (38 U.S.C. 1151). For example, a veteran goes to get spinal surgery at the VA. Due to the negligence of the VA staff, his condition is now aggravated. He has proved this to the VA and is now service - connected for payment purposes only. However, if a VA doctor warns that there will be issues post - surgery such as scarring, dizziness, fainting, etc., that is not grounds for compensation if it is an expected result of the surgery. In a second example, a veteran was pursuing training under the VA's Chapter 31 Vocational Rehabilitation and Employment program. She was receiving on - the - job training as a car mechanic. During training, a jack slipped from a car and crushed her right ankle. Disability compensation may be paid for her ankle injury because the injury occurred while she was pursuing training under a VA Vocational Rehabilitation and Employment program.

Chapter 2 "What is a Fully Developed Claim"

The Fully Developed Claim Is an Effective and Timely Procedure for Getting Results. The concept behind a Fully Developed Claim is that you will give the Regional Office every scrap of relevant and probative evidence you can get your hands on to make your case. You will provide this information up front when you make your formal application by filling out the appropriate benefit forms and including all your evidence with it. The goal is for all the evidence that you assemble to be enough for the Regional Office development team to pass on to the rating activity for a final decision. This Fully Developed Claim concept could get you a decision within a matter of a few months instead of the typical 8 to 24 months that it takes by simply applying and waiting for VA to assist you in developing your evidence.

Steps of the Fully Developed Claim Process for Disability Compensation.

Step 1. Decide Whether the Condition Warrants Making a Claim

Step 2. Submit an "Intent to File", VBA Form 21-0966

Step 3. Obtain Your Discharge and Your Own Service Treatment Records (STRs)

Step 4. Obtain Your Own Private Medical Records

Step 5. Obtain Disability Evaluations from Private Clinicians Where Possible

Step 6. Have Your Doctors/Specialists Provide Opinion Letters If Needed

Step 7. Produce Lay Statements

Step 8. Locate Records to Establish Duty Assignments Where Applicable

Step 9. Fill out the "Fully Developed Claim" Form for the Claimed Benefit

Step 10. Double Check Everything and Include Necessary Documentation

Step 11. Arrange for Representation or Third-Party Help If Needed

Step 12. Submit the Claim

Step 13. Expect Scheduling of a Compensation and Pension Examination

Step 1. Decide Whether the Condition Warrants Making a Claim

Many veterans seem to think that because of their service, they have an entitlement to disability benefits even if they aren't currently disabled. Or, if they are currently disabled, they seem to think that all their ailments are a result of being a veteran. This attitude causes several veterans or their survivors to make application thinking that VA owes them something whether they qualify are not. Unfortunately, this attitude leads to a great number of claims that are filed where there is no benefit. It is also unfortunate that many people with this attitude come away from their experience with a denial with a bad taste in their mouth and a distrust of VA.

Step 2. Submit an "Intent to File", VBA Form 21-0966

Once you feel that you can justify a claim for benefits and not waste your time or VA's time, you should proceed to submit an "Intent to File." An "Intent to File," before March of 2015, was known as an "informal claim" for benefits. The "Intent to File" allows you to notify your Regional Office that you will be submitting a substantially complete claim with the appropriate claims form in order to start the process at some future date. You have one year from filing an "Intent to File" for filing the formal application for a substantially complete claim. Most importantly, the "Intent to File" will establish an effective date for back-pay purposes. The effective date with be the first day of the month following receipt of the "Intent to File.".

The effective date governs the date of payment for benefits. For example, if your effective date is July 15, 2018 and the application gets approved on November 10, 2018, you will receive two payments by deposit. The first is a lump sum back-payment dating back to and starting on August 1, 2018 for the months of August, September, and October. The second payment will be the first of the monthly payments. The monthly payment, in this example, will be deposited on or around November 1, 2018. VA pays in arrears so this payment will represent October's benefit.

Step 3. Obtain Your Discharge and Your Own Service Treatment Records (STR)

Neither the scanning center nor the Regional Office is set up to return your original discharge to you. They will destroy your original copy.

If your claim is going to be tied to service treatment records, then you should use Form SF 180 to get those records from the Service Center in St. Louis. This does not mean that the Regional Office would not order these for you, it just may take them two or three months to get around to it. Go ahead and get them up front as part of the evidence collection you will be doing for your Fully Developed Claim.

Health records cover the outpatient, dental and mental health treatment that former members received while in military service. Health records include induction and separation physical examinations, as well as routine medical care (doctor/dental visits, lab tests, etc.) when the patient was not admitted to a hospital.

If your discharge or medical records were destroyed in the fire at the records center in St. Louis, your state Department of Veterans Affairs may have a copy of that in their archives. Many states provide this service to veterans who were discharged in their home state. Find your state Department of Veterans Affairs online and contact them. You can also contact one of the private research firms that specializes in military records to research the archives in Washington DC of the various military services, especially if you are trying to establish more than just a copy of your discharge.

Step 4. Obtain Your Own Private Medical Records

As part of the Fully Developed Claim process, you should order your own personal medical records. Your doctors and specialists are used to being paid a fee to provide copies of your records to third-party organizations. Sometimes these copy fees can be as much as $100 or more.

"Medical Records Request." We have found that the regional medical centers are quite responsive to individual requests, and if you want the records yourself, they will send them to you in digital form on a CD within about a month after your submitting the request.

VA Form 10-5345 – Request for and Authorization to Release Medical Records

VA Form 10-5345a – Individual's Request for a Copy of Their Own Health Information

Step 5. Obtain Disability Evaluations from Private Clinicians Where Possible

For many of the presumptive service-connected conditions such as cancer, heart disease, diabetes and other chronic diseases or disorders, description of the disease process, symptoms and past and current treatment protocols are enough to guide the rating activity to assign a level of disability. Debilitating diseases are already inherently disabling. Your private medical records might be enough for the rater to make a decision on the claim. On the other hand, some conditions or diseases need a level of disability to be determined in order to make a rating decision. This is especially, true for conditions involving range of motion limitations, requirements for assistance from others and cognitive impairment.

It is important for you to establish your own line of evidence and not rely on VA to provide all the evidence for your disability or your service connection. Whether the application you are making is presumptive service-connected or not, you should try to furnish your own private disability evaluation.

Step 6. Have Your Doctors or Specialists Provide Opinion Letters If Needed

Where your claim is for a condition for which you have no service records and for which you must rely on establishing a nexus of your current disabling condition tied to an exposure, unreported injury, unreported disease or other incident incurred in the service, you will have to establish – through a clinical opinion – which a service connection exists. This will almost always require an expert opinion from a doctor or psychiatrist or psychologist or social worker or perhaps an optician that the current condition is likely a result of that incident incurred in the service. If you do not provide this evidence, the Regional Office will either try to infer from your other nonmedical evidence that it is service-connected, or VA may likely order and Opinion Examination with the request that the examiner offer an opinion on the service connection.

If you rely entirely on VA to help you establish the service connection, you have a higher probability of losing the contest. If the Regional Office insists on ordering an opinion, you must provide your own offsetting private opinion of the service connection in case the rating authority in the Regional Office – based on the opinion of its own examiner – decides that your current condition is not service-connected.

If you need to prove service connection, do the following. When you have your disability examination with your private doctor or specialist or both, ask them for this expert opinion on the service connection. Of course, you will have to provide them with the details and these details must be in the opinion letter they produce for you. You must give them these written details when you show up for your examination. You must write out these details exactly as you will give them to VA in your own sworn lay statement as to what was incurred in service. The background information your doctor is using must concur with what you are telling VA. The more detailed the explanation in the opinion letter, the better the evidence. Explain to private medical examiners the importance of this opinion.

Your medical examiners should use the following terminology in determining whether, in their expert opinion, the current condition is tied to the incident incurred in the service based on your written description that will be inserted in the letter.

"Is due to"

(Examiner is 100% sure that the current disability condition was incurred as a result of illness, injury or exposure in service);

"More likely than not"

(Examiner feels there is a greater than 50% probability that the current disability condition was incurred as a result of illness, injury or exposure in service);

"At least as likely as not"

(examiner feels there is an equal to or greater than 50% probability that the current disability condition was incurred as a result of illness, injury or exposure in service);

"Not at least as likely as not"

(Examiner feels there is less than a 50% probability that the current disability condition was incurred as a result of illness, injury or exposure in service)

Oftentimes your clinician is unwilling to provide a definitive opinion that the current medical condition is a result of the service connection you are claiming. You may find it easier to convince the clinician to offer a less definitive guesstimate that there is only 50-50 chance or greater the current disability is service-connected. This may seem more reasonable to the examining practitioner. The opinion provider will use the words that the current disability is "at least as likely as not" to have been incurred in the service based on information provided by the you and a review of the medical record. The clinician has opined that there is a "roll of the dice" chance or greater it was incurred in service and if VA has no evidence to the contrary – under the doctrine of reasonable doubt (38 CFR 3.102) – you will receive an award.

Sometimes, with the permission of your treating specialist or clinician, you can write the opinion letter yourself and then ask your professional provider to okay, edit and sign the opinion that you have written. This often works well when you work together with the nurse, medical student or other staff member of your professional to read your lay statements, decipher any medical literature you have provided and then prepare the letter for the doctor to sign.

Step 7. Produce Lay Statements

For many claims, persuasive lay evidence, especially that provided by statements from the claimant, is essential for obtaining an award.

Step 8. Locate Records to Establish Duty Assignments Where Applicable

Standard Form 180 (SF 180), is used to request copies of records from the Records Management Center, in St. Louis, Missouri. The following records are kept there unless they were destroyed by the fire.

DD 214

Service treatment records

Personnel records

Step 9 Fill out the "Fully Developed Claim" Form for the Claimed Benefit

There are also some forms that will accompany a 526 EZ such as those for PTSD, sexual assault and status of dependents.

You must be very careful that you submit all the evidence that is needed to make a decision with the initial application. If you go back and submit additional evidence – whether VA requests, it or not – you will lose the special tracking of the Fully Developed Claim and your claim will revert to the standard track slow down the process considerably. As a result of losing special handling, the process could end up taking forever as many of these "standard" claims do.

To avoid losing special treatment is why it is so important to file an "Intent to File" first. An "Intent to File" is not considered a substantially complete claim, and VA will not start any process on it until the Regional Office gets your formal claim application with all the information for a Fully Developed Claim. The "Intent to File" will establish a payment date while at the same time allowing you to gather all the evidence you need. The clock starts ticking with the actual adjudication process when you submit the full application package.

Don't assume that there will be a final decision when filing an FDC. With some claims, the rating authority may order a medical evaluation from veterans' health care or from a contracting organization that does these types of exams. On the other hand, priority treatment as a Fully Developed Claim will often result in that special examination being ordered perhaps within a matter of weeks of receiving the initial application.

VA Form 26-526 EZ does not include information for a spouse or other dependents. If the benefit you are applying for or anticipating includes payment for having a spouse or dependents – such as SMC – then you need to include VA Form 21-686c – Declaration of Status of Dependents with your application.

Step 10. Double Check Everything and Include Necessary Documentation

Make sure all pertinent boxes on your application are filled out or if they are not applicable put "N/A" in them. If you are submitting application for a benefit that pays an award that includes dependents, answer all questions pertaining to marriage, dependents and relationships on VA Form VA Form 21-686c – Declaration of Status of Dependents. If you cannot provide places and dates you can sometimes estimate them or if you cannot you must provide copies of marriage certificates or the equivalent

Forms for Representation for Assistance

VA Form 21-22a – Appointment of Individual a Claimant's Representative

VA Form 21-0845 – Authorization to Disclose Personal Information to a Third Party

Step 11. Submit the Claim In order to improve timeliness and reduce the cost of scanning claims into the Veterans Benefits Management System (VBMS), VA has implemented Centralized Mail Processing (CMP). Under these new procedures, claimants and beneficiaries should now send all mail directly to the scanning vendor (Janesville, Wisconsin Intake Center), eliminating the need for Regional Office (RO) or Pension Management Center (PMC) mail processing.

Step 12. Expect scheduling of Compensation/ Pension Examination

A Compensation and Pension examination (C&P) may be ordered for your claim. The Fully Developed Claim system incorporates "Disability Benefits Questionnaires" that VA encourages you to use with your private physician to turn in with your application. You should always use a privately produced DBQ where that is possible. If it is not possible, you should allow the Regional Office to order an exam to do a DBQ assessment. This should not interfere with the priority of your FDC claim and will not take it off track.

Step 13. What to Do If the Claimant Dies before the Claim Is Adjudicated

Here are the current rules governing what happens if a claim decision is not made and the claimant dies.

38 USC §5121. Payment of certain accrued benefits upon death of a beneficiary

(a) Except as provided in sections 3329 and 3330 of title 31, periodic monetary benefits (other than insurance and servicemen's indemnity) under laws administered by the Secretary to which an individual was entitled at death under existing ratings or decisions or those based on evidence in the file at date of death (hereinafter in this section and section 5122 of this title referred to as "accrued benefits") and due and unpaid, shall, upon the death of such individual be paid as follows:

(1) Upon the death of a person receiving an apportioned share of benefits payable to a veteran, all or any part of such benefits to the veteran or to any other dependent or dependents of the veteran, as may be determined by the Secretary.

(2) Upon the death of a veteran, to the living person first listed below:

(A) The veteran's spouse.

(B) The veteran's children (in equal shares).

(C) The veteran's dependent parents (in equal shares).

(3) Upon the death of a surviving spouse or remarried surviving spouse, to the children of the deceased veteran.

(4) Upon the death of a child, to the surviving children of the veteran who are entitled to death Compensation, dependency and indemnity Compensation, or Death Pension.

(5) Upon the death of a child claiming benefits under chapter 18 of this title, to the surviving parents.

(6) In all other cases, only so much of the accrued benefits may be paid as may be necessary to reimburse the person who bore the expense of last sickness and burial.

(b) No part of any accrued benefits shall be used to reimburse any political subdivision of the United States for expenses incurred in the last sickness or burial of any beneficiary.

(c) Applications for accrued benefits must be filed within one year after the date of death. If a claimant's application is incomplete at the time it is originally submitted, the Secretary shall notify the claimant of the evidence necessary to complete the application. If such evidence is not received within one year from the date of such notification, no accrued benefits may be paid.

If you read this law carefully, it says that evidence had to be on file at the time of death to determine a decision on the application. We are not sure, but we think that VA has found it convenient to say that regardless of what was in the claims file at the time of death, there is no benefit at the death of the claimant. Whether this is just convenient to avoid processing the claim or whether it is common, we do not know. Prior to the substitution law, it was commonly accepted that "the claim – and thus the benefit – died with the claimant."

There must also be someone in the line of succession to receive the residual benefit – called accrued benefit – that would have been paid to the death of the claimant. This is either a spouse or children. For purposes of veteran's benefits, a child is defined as a minor age 18 or less, a full-time student age 23 or less, any other child age 30 or less who is also a veteran or a child any age who became totally dependent prior to age 18.

There is no option to pay to the estate of the claimant. Therefore, if there are no individuals in the line of succession, there is no benefit. In this case, the benefit becomes an "accrued benefit for final costs" and the amount that would have been owing, if the application had been approved, could be used to pay for the out-of-pocket expenses of the person or persons who bore the expense of last sickness and burial or for just debts. When there is a surviving spouse, application for an accrued benefit for final costs.

VA Form 21-534EZ – Application for DIC, Death Pension, and or Accrued Benefits

Where there is no surviving spouse, application final costs are made using the following form.

VA Form 21-601 – Application for Accrued Amounts due a Deceased Beneficiary

The claim dying with the claimant was the situation prior to 2008 when Congress passed legislation allowing for someone to step in and take over the claim. This substitution can only take effect if there is someone in the line of succession to inherit the benefit from the first day of the month following the effective date to the month of death. For most senior veterans, there will be no children in the line of succession unless an adult child became totally dependent prior to age 18. Here is the new law. The right of substitution applies to original claims and to claims on appeal.

38 USC §5121A. Substitution in case of death of claimant

(a) Substitution.—(1) If a claimant dies while a claim for any benefit under a law administered by the Secretary, or an appeal of a decision with respect to such a claim, is pending, a living person who would be eligible to receive accrued benefits due to the claimant under section 5121(a) of this title may, not later than one year after the date of the death of such claimant, file a request to be substituted as the claimant for the purposes of processing the claim to completion.

(2) Any person seeking to be substituted for the claimant shall present evidence of the right to claim such status within such time as prescribed by the Secretary in regulations.

(3) Substitution under this subsection shall be in accordance with such regulations as the Secretary may prescribe.

Chapter 3 What is this Special Monthly Compensation, and do I qualify? "

Special Monthly Compensation is a tax - free benefit paid in addition to the regular VA Disability Compensation, to a veteran who, because of military service, incurred the loss or loss of use of specific organs or extremities. You can qualify for SMC if you have : loss , or loss of use , of a hand or foot ; immobility of a joint or paralysis ; loss of sight of an eye (having only light perception) ; loss , or loss of use , of a reproductive organ ; complete loss , or loss of use , of both buttocks ; deafness of both ears (having absence of air and bone conduction) ; inability to communicate by speech (complete organic aphonia) ; loss of a percentage of tissue from a single breast , or both breasts , from mastectomy or radiation treatment . Also, if you are service connected at the 100 % rate for a single condition, while your other conditions total 60 % or more, you are eligible to receive an SMC award.

In addition to compensation based on the degree of disability, Congress has also authorized additional compensation for certain disabilities. This "special monthly compensation" ("SMC") is intended to compensate claimants for service-connected conditions that involve loss of use or anatomical loss (amputation) of body parts, such as hands or feet, or loss of hearing or sight. SMC can result in significantly more monthly compensation for severely injured veterans.

While a scheduler rating depends on the severity of a condition, SMC for loss of use does not depend on the degree of loss, except that the loss of use must be permanent. The more seriously disabled veteran may be eligible for SMC payments for combinations of anatomical loss or loss of use. In addition, severely disabled veterans may be awarded further compensation for regular aid and attendance needs and for permanent housebound conditions. As SMC has many possible combinations and involves a significant amount of additional compensation

Levels of SMC Ratings

Each level of SMC ratings is successive and are preceded by an entitlement to certain conditions included under SMC (K). The basic elements of Special Monthly Compensation ratings include:

•anatomical (or physical) loss or the loss of use (Loss of use from neurological, muscular, vascular, contractures, etc.) Of one or more of the following:

Limbs,

Hands, feet,

Reproductive organs,

Aphonia (loss of voice);

Deafness;

Blindness;

Loss of bowel and bladder control;

Being permanently housebound;

and a need for regular aid and attendance with activities of daily living or a higher level of care. All of which must be a result of the veteran's service-connected disabilities.

A rating of SMC (K) would include:

The anatomical loss or loss of use (Loss of use from neurological, muscular, vascular, contractures, etc.) of:

one hand.

one foot.

both buttocks (where the applicable bilateral muscle group prevents the individual from maintaining unaided upright posture, rising and stooping actions).

◦one or more creative organs used for reproduction (absence of testicles, ovaries or other creative organ, ¼ loss of tissue of a single breast or both breasts in combination) due to trauma while in service, or as a residual of a service-connected disability(ies). NOTE: these do not serve as eligible prerequisite conditions for the higher levels of SMC.

One eye (loss of use to include specific levels of blindness).

Complete organic aphonia (constant loss of voice due to disease)

Deafness of both ears to include absence of air and bone conduction.

A rating of SMC (L) would include:

The anatomical loss or loss of use of:

Both feet,

One hand and one foot

Blindness in both eyes with visual acuity of 5/200 and less.

Permanently bedridden.

Regular need for aid and attendance to assist with activities of daily living such as dressing oneself, tending to personal hygiene, care and adjustment of assistive appliances or prosthetics, feeding oneself, and the like. (specific criteria are established in 38 CFR § 3.352(a)) (NOTE: If such services are not being provided at the expense of the U.S. Government due to hospitalization).

Ratings above the SMC (L) level to include SMC (M), SMC (N), SMC (O), SMC (P), SMC(R) and SMC(S) are specialized multifaceted levels which are based on various specific combinations of anatomical loss or loss of use of designated extremities and/or senses, together with seriously disabling conditions and particular degrees of aid and attendance requirements, housebound or bedridden statuses deemed medically necessary, and explicit service-connection ratings. These levels also outline various requirements to include full and half step upgraded SMC level ratings. The conditions providing the basis of these levels are as follows.

A rating of SMC (M) would include:

- The anatomical loss or loss of use of (neurological loss):
  - Both hands,
  - Both legs at the region of the knee
  - One arm at the region of the elbow with one leg at the region of the knee
- Blindness in both eyes having only light perception.
- Blindness in both eyes resulting in the need for regular aid and attendance.

A rating of SMC (N) would include:

- The anatomical loss or loss of use of both arms at the region of the elbow.
- The anatomical loss of both legs so near the hip that it prevents the use of a prosthetic appliance.
- The anatomical loss of one arm so near the shoulder that it prevents the use of a prosthetic appliance along with the anatomical loss of one leg so near the hip that it prevents the use of a prosthetic appliance.
- The anatomical loss of both eyes and blindness in both eyes to include loss of light perception.

A rating of SMC (O) would include:

- The anatomical loss of both arms so near the shoulder that it prevents the use of a prosthetic appliance.
- Bilateral deafness rated at least 60 percent disabling along with service-connected blindness with visual acuity of 20/200 or less of both eyes.

- Complete deafness in one ear or bilateral deafness rated at least 40 percent disabling along with service-connected blindness in both eyes to include loss of light perception.

- Paraplegia – paralysis of both lower extremities along with bowel and bladder incontinence.

- Helplessness due to a combination of anatomical loss or loss of use or two extremities with deafness and blindness or a combination of multiple injuries causing severe and total disability.

A rating of SMC (P) would include:

- The anatomical loss or loss of use of a leg at or below the knee along with the anatomical loss or loss of use of the other leg at a level above the knee.

- The anatomical loss or loss of use of a leg below the knee along with the anatomical loss or loss of use of an arm above the elbow.

- The anatomical loss or loss of use of one leg above the knee and the anatomical loss or loss of use of a hand.

- Blindness in both eyes meeting the requirements outlined in SMC (L), (M) or (N) levels.

A rating of SMC(R):

Ratings under SMC(R) are assigned for seriously disabled veterans in need of advanced levels of aid and attendance.

SMC(R) ratings require a minimal combination of entitlement to both SMC (O) and SMC (L). Additionally, Veterans in receipt of SMC rates based on Aid and Attendance are strongly advised to contact their service representative and/or VA Regional Office should they become hospitalized at the expense of the U.S. Government (i.e. a VA medical facility) as failure to do so could create an overpayment of monetary benefits.

A rating of SMC(S):

Ratings under SMC(S) are also available if the veteran is permanently housebound. The VA defines "permanently housebound" as being substantially (as opposed to completely) confined to a dwelling as the result of service-connected disability and it is reasonably certain that that such disability will continue throughout the veteran's lifetime. These kinds of determinations should be made by a physician, whose written opinions or reports in this respect would serve as the best evidence to submit in support of a claim for "s" SMC benefits.

A rating of SMC (T): Traumatic Brain Injury

Ratings under SMC(T) are available to veterans who need regular aid A&A for residuals of Traumatic Brain Injury (TBI) but is not eligible for a higher level of A&A under (R)(2), and would require hospitalization, nursing home care, or other residential institutional care in absence of regular in-home aid and attendance.

Chapter 4 "What is a Clear and Unmistakable Error (CUE)"

If the VA finds that they have made a mistake in giving you a rating that they should not have, they can sever your benefits regardless of how long you have been receiving compensation. If you find that they have made a Clear and Unmistakable Error (CUE), you can challenge that error. Keep in mind that a review for a clear and unmistakable error in a prior board decision must be based on the record and the law that existed when that decision was made (except for the Nehmer Law). Also, to warrant revision of a board decision on the grounds of clear and unmistakable error, there must have been an error in the board's adjudication of the appeal which, had it not been made, would have manifestly changed the outcome when it was made. Examples that are NOT considered CUE's are: A new medical diagnosis that "corrects" an earlier diagnosis considered in a board decision, the Secretary's failure to fulfill the duty to assist, and disagreements as to how the facts were weighed or evaluated. Filing a CUE sounds simple enough but can be difficult based on many factors. In a reverse situation, the VA noticed a veteran was in receipt of compensation for a personality disorder after she had decided to file for Special Home Adaptation (SHA). Note: Whenever you open a claim, all of your current service - connected disabilities are subject to adjudication. She did not qualify SHA and was not supposed to be service connected for her narcissistic personality disorder. Her compensation was severed completely as her personality disorder (which was not superimposed upon) was the only disability she was service connected for. Intellectual disability (intellectual developmental disorder) and personality disorders are not diseases or injuries for compensation purposes. If you strongly believe that the VA missed an SMC award or another mistake has been made, consult a representative first to assist you through the process and so that they can identify whether it is a legitimate mistake.

Chapter 5 "What is DIC?"

There is something called Death and Indemnity Compensation (DIC). It is a tax - free monetary benefit paid to eligible survivors of military service members who died in the line of duty or eligible survivors of veterans whose death resulted from a service - related injury or disease. DIC," is available to eligible survivors and dependents of veterans who had service-connected disabilities or diseases. The amount of DIC compensation is not based on income and is paid as a tax-free monthly benefit.

To be considered a qualifying veteran for DIC purposes, the deceased veteran must meet either of the following criteria:

Died from a service-related injury or disease

Died from a non-service-related injury or disease but was eligible for or receiving VA compensation for a totally disabling service-connected disability: For at least 10 years before death, or For at least 1 year if the veteran was a former POW who died after 9/30/1999, For at least 5 years and immediately following discharge from active duty

To be eligible for DIC, a surviving spouse must meet any of the following criteria:

Married to the veteran before 1/1/1957

Married the veteran within 15 years of discharge from the period of service during which the service-connected disability or disease occurred or was made worse

Married to the veteran for at least a year OR had a child with the veteran AND lived with them until their death

In all cases, the spouse must not be remarried, unless they are over the age of 57 and were remarried on or after 12/16/2003.

To be eligible for DIC, a surviving child must meet all the following criteria:

Under the age of 18, or under the age of 23 if attending school Unmarried

not factored into a surviving spouse/parent's DIC

Children who cannot live independently due to a disability may also be eligible for DIC benefits.

Several factors will increase a surviving spouse's DIC benefits amount, including:

If the veteran had been receiving disability compensation for a totally disabling service-connected disability or disease for at least 8 continuous years during which the surviving spouse was married to them

Any dependent children under the age of 18

If the surviving spouse is entitled to aid and attendance (A&A)

If the surviving spouse is entitled to housebound financial assistance

Limitations on DIC Compensation

If a survivor receives any compensation that the veteran was receiving or entitled to after the date of the veteran's death, they will be required to pay that money back if they spend it.

If a survivor is eligible for payments under the Survivor Benefit Plan (SBP), those payments will be reduced by the amount of DIC benefits received.

Parents' Dependency and Indemnity Compensation

Parents of veterans who died as the result of a service-related injury or disease may be eligible to receive a tax-free monthly benefit if their income falls below a certain level.

"Parents" for DIC purposes include biological, adoptive, and foster parents.

If eligible parents are married, they must report their spouse's income as well, even if their spouse is not also a parent of the deceased veteran.

Note: The VA does not recognize common law marriage in states that do not recognize common law marriage which is most states. There have been cases where the deceased was legally married (but separated) to one woman while cohabitating with another on a long - term basis. There were also cases where a widow (er) was already being compensated through DIC and attempted to get it from a second deceased spouse simultaneously. That is not allowed even if you meet the above criteria. A lot of variables can disqualify a surviving spouse from receiving DIC if issues are not handled ahead of time.

Chapter 6 "What is an appeal, and how long the process is?"

Currently, the appellate process can be incredibly long and stressful. However, it is sometimes necessary depending on the complexities of the claim. Currently, there are "solutions" in the works to minimize the current wait time and to re - vamp the appeals process. I would advise to never attempt an appeal without the assistance of an accredited representative. The odds of winning increase dramatically if you have a knowledgeable representative to guide you. If you feel you did not receive a fair rating, there is a reason and a law behind that decision which can be best explained by a representative. Sometimes, a reconsideration can rectify the disagreement with the addition of new material evidence. A reconsideration is quicker than the 740 - 800-day turnaround time an average appeal takes assuming one opted to go through the Decision Review Officer (DRO) review process versus the traditional appellate review process which takes 5 - 7 years at the time this was written. Wait times are expected to change very soon. To start the appellate process after a denial, you would first file a Notice of Disagreement (NOD). You have one year from the decision to do this. After the VA receives and processes this, you will receive something called a Statement of the Case (SOC) which is an explanation of the decision made on your case. An SOC provides the veteran with a complete understanding of the decision so they can prepare an effective substantive appeal with specific allegations of errors of fact or law. If you disagree with the SOC, you fill out a VA form 9 which is a substantive appeal form. You only have 60 days to fill form 9 from the date on the SOC. Normally, at this point, your claim likely requires additional evidence. I would make sure all the evidence is collected and submitted in a timely fashion. There is a lot that goes on during this process, and it takes time. Try your best to be patient throughout the process.

Chapter 7 "What is Individual Unemployability?"

Individual Unemployability (IU) is a unique part of VA's disability compensation program. It allows VA to pay certain Veterans compensation at the 100 percent rate, even though VA has not rated their service-connected disabilities at that level.

Who Is Eligible for Individual Unemployability?

- You must be a Veteran.

- You must be unable to hold a job as a result of service-connected disabilities. This means maintaining substantially gainful employment. (VA considers odd jobs as marginal employment. They do not affect your eligibility for IU.)

- You must have either:

  - One disability that is rated at 60 percent or more

- Multiple disabilities, with one disability rated at 40 percent or higher, and a total rating of 70 percent or more.

What Are the Evidence Requirements?

- You must have evidence of at least one service-connected disability that meets the above scheduler requirements.

- You must prove the service-connected disability or disabilities alone prevent getting or keeping substantially gainful employment. This can be due to inability to perform either mental or physical tasks.

There are certain circumstances where this benefit may be granted with a lower disability rating than required. Evidence must show that applying the normal requirements is unreasonable. Examples that may be considered include major interference with employment and frequent hospitalizations. These are considered on a case by case bases.

Chapter 8 "How do I file for Military Sexual Assault with no proof?"

The VA defines Military Sexual Trauma (MST) as sexual assault (including rape) or repetitive, threatening sexual harassment. Some find themselves affected by their experiences from the time they occurred, or many years later may develop psychological and physical issues. You cannot receive compensation based on military sexual trauma alone. You must have a compensable health condition, usually a mental disorder. There is a significant stigma against reporting such assaults, and assaults are often not reported right away and sometimes, there is no record of the incident at all because the military never investigated. The VA understands this and does not require that service medical records contain proof of the assault or harassment. That word "require" can be tricky. While they may not require a police report or letter from the command corroborating what happened, the VA will accept other forms of proof. Statements from your friends in service, family members, counselors, or clergy, or proof of behavioral changes such as evidence of a drug or alcohol problem occurring after the incident may be used to substantiate the case further. Changes in job performance and / or changes in social or economic behavior for which there is no other explanation along with marital and / or sexual difficulties can also be used as proof. If you have a claim for an MST (due to PTSD or other mental disorder), a statement in support of a claim for service connection for Post - Traumatic Stress Disorder Secondary to Personal Assault is to be filled out. Note: Even though the VA does not require veterans to submit evidence, MST claims are often denied without it. It can be a tough battle to receive a service connection for this without viable evidence. Women and men in the service who have reported sexual assault by another service member and have been medically discharged for a personality disorder have been denied VA benefits on that basis. If you received a medical discharge due to a personality disorder, you can apply to have your reason for discharge changed so that you can obtain benefits. For example, you can seek your diagnosis changed from personality disorder to post - traumatic stress disorder. That process will take time, but it will be well worth it in the long run if approved.

Chapter 9 "How can I receive my DD - 214" You will not be able to receive benefits in most places without your DD-214. In order to retrieve a copy of your DD - 214, separation documents , or anything that was in your Official Military Personnel File (OMPF) and medical records , go to https : / / www.archives.gov /

veterans / military - service - records . Most files are not available online. They receive on average 4,000 to 5,000 requests per day and the wait time may be lengthy, but according to the site, they are responding to requests for separation documents within 10 days about 92 % of the time. Depending on which documents you require, there may be a fee. After 10 days, you will be able to check the status of your request. More information is located on the site.

Conclusion

The Veterans Benefits Administration (VBA) offer many benefits from disability compensation, burial, disability pension, survivor benefits, medical benefits, and education benefits. The focus of this book was to provide an overview of some of the questions that many veterans ask daily. VA law is practice that has accomplish many milestones, however there is still room to improve. If you got questions on veteran benefits or not getting the assistance you need to file your claim, there are many options available to assist you nationwide.

I am a VA Accredited Claims agent who served many years in the United States Army. I am an OIF veteran. I currently reside in Georgia. I established my own veteran organization, VOICE4VETS, LLC to aim at providing proper advice and guidance to veterans and their families. If you have any questions on VA benefits or want me to be your agent contact me at voice4vets@gmail.com.

ONE VETERAN HELPING ANOTHER

www.ingramcontent.com/pod-product-compliance
Lightning Source LLC
Chambersburg PA
CBHW081148170526

45158CB00009BA/2769